SEE-THROUGH

STORMS

GILL PAUL
ILLUSTRATED BY **JULIAN BAKER** AND **JANET BAKER**

RUNNING PRESS
KIDS

9   8   7   6   5   4   3   2   1
Digit on the right indicates the number
of this printing

Library of Congress
Control Number: 2005938635

ISBN-13: 978-0-7624-2662-1
ISBN-10: 0-7624-2662-4

This book was created by
THE IVY PRESS LIMITED
The Old Candlemakers
West Street, Lewes BN7 2NZ

CREATIVE DIRECTOR Peter Bridgewater
PUBLISHER Jason Hook
EDITORIAL DIRECTOR Caroline Earle
SENIOR PROJECT EDITOR Hazel Songhurst
ART DIRECTOR Sarah Howerd
DESIGNER Wayne Blades
ILLUSTRATORS Julian Baker and Janet Baker

This book may be ordered by mail from the
publisher. Please include $2.50 for postage and
handling. But try your bookstore first!

Running Press Book Publishers
125 South Twenty-Second Street
Philadelphia, Pennsylvania 19103-4399

Visit us on the web!
www.runningpress.com

CONTENTS

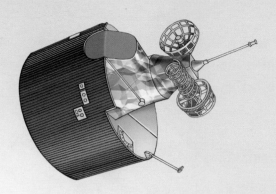

INTRODUCTION

There seems to be a weather story in the news almost every day, whether it's drought in Africa, flooding in India, hurricanes in the Caribbean, or ice storms in Canada. What causes these weather extremes, and why do they occur so often? One of the main things that affects weather on earth is the strength of the sun's rays, which are strongest at the Equator, where the sun is directly overhead, and weakest at the North and South Poles, where the sun is low in the sky. Other features of our planet also affect the climate, including oceans, mountains, forests, and deserts. We live in a diverse world, with many different weather systems—and it's where these systems meet that trouble often starts.

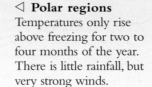

◁ **Polar regions**
Temperatures only rise above freezing for two to four months of the year. There is little rainfall, but very strong winds.

SUMMER

WINTER

CHANGING SEASONS
The earth's axis is tilted at an angle of 23.5° and this is what causes our seasons. As the earth moves in orbit around the sun, the northern hemisphere leans toward the sun from April to September, causing warm summer weather, and away from it from October to March, causing winter.

23.5°

NORTH POLE

△ **Northern regions**
Areas such as northern Canada, Scandinavia, and Russia have harsh weather for up to nine months a year and a short summer.

NIGHT AND DAY
The earth turns on its axis, an imaginary line joining the poles, once every 24 hours. When your area faces the sun it's day, and when it faces away it's night. Nighttime temperatures are cooler than daytime ones, although areas with a lot of trees keep their warmth better.

The earth turns on its axis every 24 hours

SOUTH POLE

△ **Tropical regions**
Warm weather all year round; heavy rainfall and frequent thunderstorms.

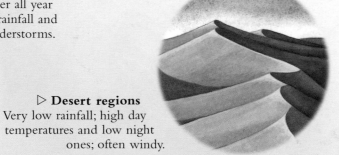

▷ **Desert regions**
Very low rainfall; high day temperatures and low night ones; often windy.

The earth's axis, at 23.5° to perpendicular

▷ **Temperate regions**
Four seasons; warm summers; snowy winters; moderate rainfall.

▷ **Mountain regions**
At higher altitudes there is more rain, wind, and snow, and lower temperatures than in the surrounding lowland areas.

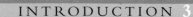

WHAT CAUSES STORMS?

The hottest areas of the planet tend to be between the Tropic of Cancer (23.5° north of the Equator) and the Tropic of Capricorn (23.5° south of the Equator), while the coldest regions are at the poles. The atmosphere and the oceans are constantly trying to equalize this heat, by transferring hot air masses and warm ocean currents from the tropics to the polar regions and sending colder air and waters back from the poles to the tropics. The movement of air masses creates differences in air pressure, which in turn create winds. The bigger the difference, the stronger the winds. Fast-moving low-pressure systems create changeable weather, while high pressure tends to bring stable weather.

MAPPING WEATHER

Weather fronts are shown as lines (known as isobars) with triangles indicating the direction of travel of a cold front and semicircles showing the direction of a warm front. Isobars link points with the same atmospheric pressure—either low or high.

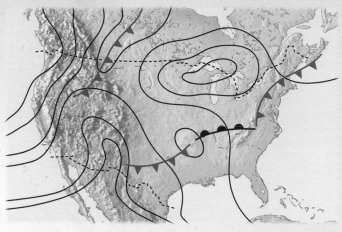

△ **Riding the jet stream**
Pilots flying airplanes from the U.S. to northern Europe frequently hitch a ride on a northerly jet stream (*see right*) that can increase their speed by up to 100 miles per hour (160 km/hr).

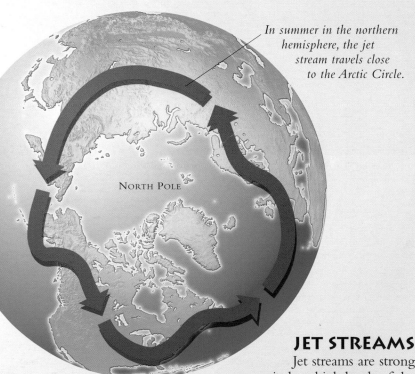

In summer in the northern hemisphere, the jet stream travels close to the Arctic Circle.

NORTH POLE

△ **Cold air chase**
When a fast-moving cold front catches up with a slow-moving warm front, it pushes the warm air mass upward.

COLD FRONT

warm air forced up

WARM FRONT

cool air

WEATHER FRONTS

The boundary between two air masses with different characteristics (e.g., in air temperature or humidity) is called a weather front.

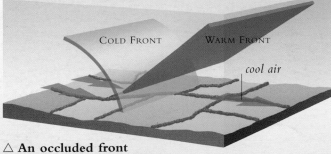

COLD FRONT   WARM FRONT

cool air

△ **An occluded front**
The two fronts travel together with the warm front above, forming an occluded front that causes unsettled weather.

JET STREAMS

Jet streams are strong winds at high levels of the atmosphere, 30,000–35,000 feet (9,000–10,700 meters). Traveling as fast as 180 miles per hour (290 km/hr), they often steer low-pressure systems. In winter they are stronger and nearer the Equator; in summer, they are weaker and nearer the poles. The more northerly the jet stream in spring, the better the coming summer. If it's further south, a rainy summer is likely.

MOVING AIR MASSES

Warm, humid air rises at the Equator, then sinks again at around 30°N and 30°S. Meanwhile, polar air masses are heading to the Equator, with some circling around about 60° latitude and the rest continuing toward the tropics.

THE DOLDRUMS

There is a static low-pressure belt around the Equator, an area known by sailors as "the doldrums." There is hardly any wind, so sailing ships can get stuck there.

TOP WEATHERMAN

Galileo Galilei (1564–1642)

- Galileo was an Italian mathematician and astronomer who was way ahead of his time. He invented the very first thermometer (or thermoscope, as he called it), and he was also the first scientist to realize that air has weight. You can prove this if you weigh a glass jar filled with air, then compare it with the weight of the same jar from which the air has been removed, leaving a vacuum.

- One of Galileo's pupils, Evangelista Torricello, was the inventor of the barometer, an instrument which measures air pressure.

Torricello filled a long glass tube with mercury and turned the open end into a dish of mercury. The height of the column that remained in the tube showed the air pressure.

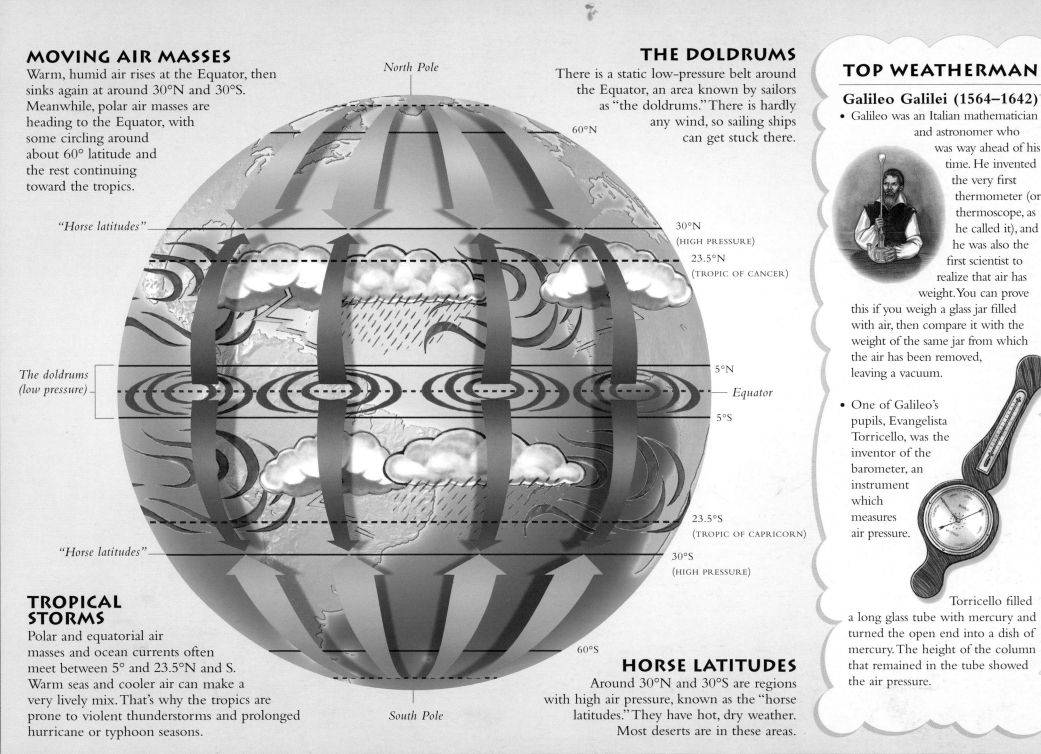

North Pole

60°N

"Horse latitudes"

30°N
(HIGH PRESSURE)

23.5°N
(TROPIC OF CANCER)

5°N

The doldrums
(low pressure)

Equator

5°S

23.5°S
(TROPIC OF CAPRICORN)

"Horse latitudes"

30°S
(HIGH PRESSURE)

60°S

South Pole

TROPICAL STORMS

Polar and equatorial air masses and ocean currents often meet between 5° and 23.5°N and S. Warm seas and cooler air can make a very lively mix. That's why the tropics are prone to violent thunderstorms and prolonged hurricane or typhoon seasons.

HORSE LATITUDES

Around 30°N and 30°S are regions with high air pressure, known as the "horse latitudes." They have hot, dry weather. Most deserts are in these areas.

TORRENTIAL RAIN

It's not just air masses that are continually on the move. Water circulates around the planet between the oceans, clouds, land, plants, and trees. Clouds are formed when the heat of the sun causes water to evaporate. As it rises, the water vapor gradually cools, until tiny drops of water or ice crystals start to condense. Each cloud is formed from billions of these drops of water or ice crystals. The clouds swell and the droplets inside them collide to become bigger drops. When they get too big, they fall from the clouds as rain or snow. Of course, we need water to sustain crops and keep us alive—but some regions get too little rainfall, while others get a whole lot more than they can deal with.

△ Weather blockers
Mountain ranges can act as rain blockers, causing dry conditions on their leeward side—the side away from the direction of the wind. For example, the Rockies block weather coming in from the Pacific, depriving the northern plains of rain.

THE WATER CYCLE

Ninety percent of the moisture in our atmosphere evaporates from the oceans, although some also comes from lakes, rivers, and transpiration from plants and trees. Moist winds blow inland until they reach high ground, where the air is forced to rise. As it rises it cools, forming clouds, and the moisture content falls as rain or snow. Rainwater and melted snow flow off the high ground into rivers or streams. Some of this soaks into the soil and the rest flows on until it reaches the ocean again.

◁ Monsoon rains
In Southeast Asia, months of dry weather are followed by monsoon rains, when rising clouds of moisture from the Indian Ocean reach the Himalayas.

△ Inside the clouds
At high levels, clouds are made of ice crystals, while at lower levels they are water droplets. In between they can be a mixture of ice, water, and supercooled droplets, all moving up and down on air currents and colliding with each other.

▷ Evaporation
The sun heats the ocean surface causing moisture to rise and form a cloud.

▷ Desert bloom

Desert plants and animals can survive on very little moisture but will die during a severe drought. A downpour of rain brings the desert into flower.

Flash floods ▷

A short, intense fall of rain that cannot be rapidly soaked up by the soil, can result in a flash flood. On August 16, 2004, the small English village of Boscastle experienced around 8 inches (20 cm) of rain falling in the space of 12 hours. The flash flood that resulted washed cars and trees down a steep gorge to the ocean. No one died at Boscastle, but mud slides after flooding can cause large numbers of fatalities in areas that are at risk.

TROPICAL RAIN

Convectional rain, which is common near the Equator, is caused by a straightforward air and sea cycle. Skies are clear in the morning, then the intense heat of the ground causes warm, moist air to rise. High above ground, the air cools and water vapor forms huge rain clouds. The droplets fuse to form raindrops, there is a torrential downpour in the late afternoon or evening, and then the cycle begins again the next day.

◁ Return to the ocean

The rain or snow falls to the ground and flows in rivers and streams to the ocean.

TYPES OF CLOUDS

The way they are named

• There are several types, depending on the amount of moisture in the air, atmospheric stability, and wind conditions. Cirrus are thin and whispy, cumulus are fluffy, stratus are flat and layered. High-level clouds (above 16,500 feet/5,000 meters) have the prefix "cirro–" and midlevel (6,500–16,500 feet/1,980–5,000 meters) have the prefix "alto–." Nimbus means "rain-bearing," and cumulonimbus clouds stretch from low to high levels of the atmosphere.

CIRRUS   CUMULUS

CUMULONIMBUS   ALTOSTRATUS

STRATUS   ALTOCUMULUS

HIGH WINDS

Winds blow from high-pressure areas to low-pressure areas, from the Equator toward the poles, and from the poles to the Equator. However, the earth's rotation deflects them to the right in the northern hemisphere and to the left in the south; this is known as the Coriolis force. This means that winds travel clockwise around high-pressure systems in the north, and counterclockwise in the south (for the same reason, water running down a drain flows clockwise in New York and counterclockwise in Sydney, Australia). Prevailing winds mean that most weather systems in the U.S. travel from west to east—but there are exceptions to every rule, and some of them are very violent ones.

△ Trade winds
Ancient navigators were well aware that while the prevailing winds in the northern Atlantic came from the west, south of 30°N, they blew from the east. Columbus would never have reached America without these winds, which were named trade winds or "easterlies."

COLD WINDS
Local geography can cause winds to divide and funnel. The fierce mistral hurtles down the Rhône Valley in France, bringing cold, dry, very gusty conditions to the south. The bora is a northeasterly wind from the Balkan Mountains that chills the eastern Adriatic Sea in winter.

WARM WINDS
The Sahara Desert is the source of several local hot, dry winds, such as the sirocco, which blows north, and the khamsin, which can cause devastation to crops in Egypt. The chinook, which blows on the eastern side of the Rockies, and the foehn in the Swiss Alps, are warm, downslope winds that can melt snow rapidly and raise the air temperature.

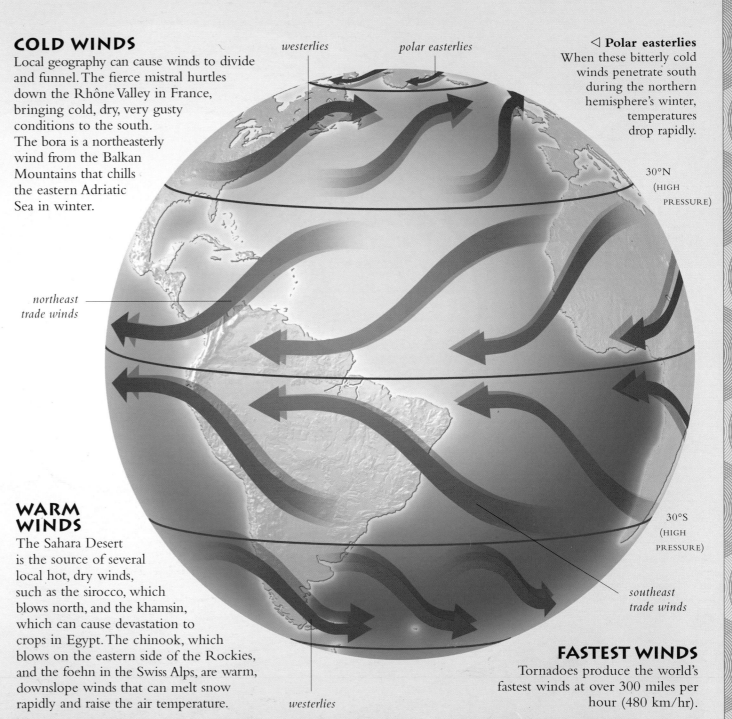

westerlies

polar easterlies

◁ **Polar easterlies**
When these bitterly cold winds penetrate south during the northern hemisphere's winter, temperatures drop rapidly.

30°N
(HIGH PRESSURE)

northeast trade winds

30°S
(HIGH PRESSURE)

southeast trade winds

westerlies

FASTEST WINDS
Tornadoes produce the world's fastest winds at over 300 miles per hour (480 km/hr).

△ Wind damage
In a high wind the greatest risk is being hit by falling trees or flying objects. The best bet is to get indoors—fast.

▽ A plague on their vacation
In 1994 a swarm of locusts arrived on the island of Lanzarote, off the African coast, on a Saharan wind.

The Beaufort scale imagery numbered 0 through 11–12.

0 1 2 3 4 5
6 7 8 9 10 11–12

△ The Beaufort Scale
This scale gives winds a rating of 0 to 12, depending on their speed: 0 is totally calm; 12 is hurricane-force winds of more than 73 miles per hour (118 km/hr). There is a separate scale for hurricanes, based on their wind speeds (*see page 20*).

WINDCHILL
Temperatures of −70°F (−57°C) or below are common in the interior of Antarctica, while wind speeds often reach well over 100 miles per hour (160 km/hr). This combined effect leads to severe windchill, causing greater heat loss from the body than the air temperature alone would suggest. For this reason, a separate windchill scale has been created. When the temperature is 10°F (−12°C), but there is a 20-mile-per hour (32 km/hr) wind, the windchill temperature is −24°F (−31°C) and there is a real risk of frostbite. In the Antarctic, when windchill is below −58°F (−50°C), exposed flesh would freeze in less than a minute.

THUNDERSTORMS

Each day there are roughly 40,000 thunderstorms around the world, and there are 2,000 raging at any given time. They are most common in tropical regions, but can also occur on warm days in temperate zones, usually in the late afternoon or early evening. The southeastern U.S., especially Florida, is very prone to them. A towering cumulonimbus cloud darkening the sky, with its top sliced into an anvil shape by high-level winds, is usually the best sign of an approaching storm—but it's also worth checking what your pet is up to. Animals are more sensitive to changes in atmospheric pressure than humans and can start behaving oddly when storms are on the way (*see page 31*).

△ **Countdown**
Count the seconds between a lightning strike and the crash of thunder to see how far away a storm is—five seconds equals 1 mile (1.6 km).

△ **Driving in lightning**
Being inside a car during a thunderstorm might be scary but it's reasonably safe, even if you get struck by lightning. The car's rubber tires provide insulation, stopping the lightning running to ground, so it will pass over the metal bodywork without harming those inside. Lightning bolts pass over aircraft in the same way.

THUNDERCLOUDS
Thunderstorms occur when the ground temperature is hotter than the air temperature. The warm, moist air rises rapidly to form cumulonimbus clouds which can be up to 12 miles (19 km) high. Different electrical charges build up inside the clouds—ice crystals at the top are generally positively charged, while water droplets, which stay at the bottom, are negatively charged, and the ground below becomes positive. With electricity, opposites attract, so when the energy has built up sufficiently, an electrical discharge runs from the negative to the positive areas—either inside the clouds or from the cloud to the ground.

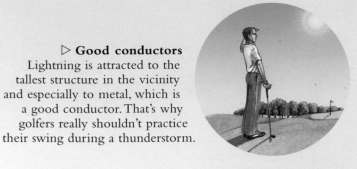

▷ **Good conductors**
Lightning is attracted to the tallest structure in the vicinity and especially to metal, which is a good conductor. That's why golfers really shouldn't practice their swing during a thunderstorm.

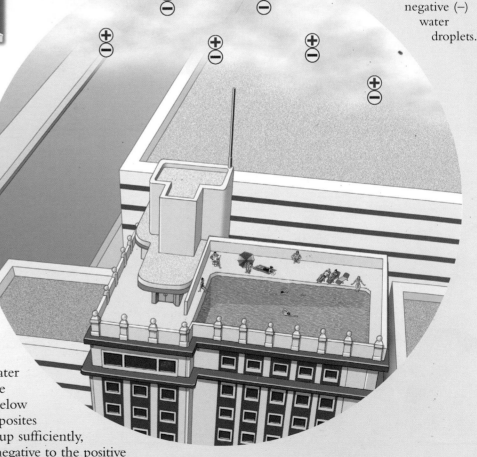

▽ **Positive and negative**
Electrical energy builds up in the cloud between the positive (+) ice crystals and negative (−) water droplets.

◁ Wildfires
Trees getting struck by lightning is a common cause of wildfires in very hot, dry areas like California, Australia, the south of France, and central Spain. One spark can turn into a raging inferno that spreads wherever the wind blows it, destroying everything in its path.

▷ Lightning rods
Metal rods are placed on the top of tall buildings to channel lightning to the ground.

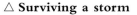
Lightning rod

LIGHTNING

The different types

- Fork and sheet are the most common types of lightning. You can see fork lightning moving from the cloud to the ground in steps. Sheet lightning lights up the whole sky close to the horizon. Ball lightning is a slow-moving ball of heat that burns out and explodes; it was first seen on top of ships' masts and called St. Elmo's Fire. Two recently discovered types of megalightning, known as Red Sprite and Blue Jet, occur up above the clouds.

RED SPRITE   BLUE JET

INTRACLOUD LIGHTNING   LIGHTNING AT SEA

FORK LIGHTNING   BALL LIGHTNING

△ Surviving a storm
If you are caught outdoors in a thunderstorm, stay away from tall trees and buildings that might attract lightning. Evidence suggests that you are more likely to survive a lightning strike if you allow your clothes to get soaked in the rain, rather than trying to stay dry.

STRIKE!
The leader stroke travels to the ground and its strike releases a huge amount of energy, creating temperatures of more than 40,000°F (22,200°C)—five times hotter than the sun! The air around it rapidly expands and contracts, causing the sound of the thunder. A brighter return stroke travels back up to the cloud, and it is this that we see as forks or sheets of lightning. The thunderstorm continues until the electrical forces have discharged—usually in one to two hours.

FREEZING STORMS

Human beings have a low tolerance for cold. Without clothes, we would start shivering at temperatures as high as 68°F (20°C). When low temperatures combine with moisture in the atmosphere, they produce a range of challenging conditions. Up in the clouds, water is either in the form of ice crystals or supercooled droplets. When these fall from the clouds through cold air onto surfaces that are below freezing point, they can create conditions that are very hazardous for humans. Blizzards, hail, and ice storms can all bring modern cities to a standstill, causing lengthy power outages and traffic chaos.

AVALANCHE!

Loose snow avalanches form when powder snow cascades down a slope. They are not nearly as dangerous as the denser slab avalanches (*see left*), which can carry chunks of hard ice, rocks, and even trees inside them. Most avalanches are caused by people climbing, skiing, or snowboarding, but a sudden warm wind that melts the surface snow can have the same effect.

A STELLAR DENDRITE
ICE CRYSTAL

SNOWFLAKES

A snowflake can be a single ice crystal or a collection of many crystals that form in clouds when water vapor freezes. The ice crystals grow into hexagonal (6–sided) forms and can be simple shapes or complex structures. A snowflake 1 inch (2.5 cm) across might be made from over 100 separate crystals, all with different patterns. When the air temperature is below freezing (32°F/0°C), snow falls as the small, powdery flakes that skiers like best. Snowflakes that form when the air is close to the freezing point will be larger and wetter.

ICE STORMS

A heavy downpour of supercooled droplets produces a glaze that can bring down power cables and tree branches, and ice up airplane wings.

▷ Structure of a hailstone

A hailstone starts out as a minute speck of salt or industrial dirt within a cloud on which water condenses to form an ice crystal. Inside cumulonimbus clouds, it is caught in updrafts and downdrafts, and each time the ice crystal touches a supercooled water droplet another layer of ice forms around it. The bigger the cloud, the more layers of ice and so the bigger the hailstone.

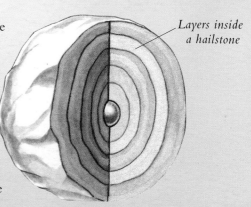

Layers inside a hailstone

FOG

Fog forms when moist air moves over cold surfaces, causing the water vapor to condense into droplets. For pilots and sailors, the official definition of fog is a visibility of less than 1,000 yards (915 meters), but car drivers will have problems when they can't see as far as 100 yards (91 meters) ahead.

▷ **Types of frost**

Weather forecasters take air temperature measurements at about 5 feet (1.5 meters) off the ground, but the ground is usually colder than the air, so you can have a ground frost (when liquid freezes) without an air frost. Black ice is a thin layer of frost on roads, which is dangerous for drivers, because it's difficult to see and very slippery. Hoarfrost is the white crust on grass or leaves when the air cools and water condenses.

AIR FROST

BLACK ICE

HOARFROST

MEGAHAIL

The dangers of hailstones

- Most hailstones are ½ to ¾ inch (1.25–2 cm) across.
- The largest hailstones form in the tropics, and can be as big as golf balls.
- In the U.S., the area from the Rockies to the Mississippi, between Texas and Montana, is known as "Hail Alley."
- The largest hailstone ever recorded in the U.S. fell in Aurora, Nebraska, on June 22, 2003. It was 7½ inches (19 cm) across.

◁ **Blizzards**

Blizzards occur when there are winds of more than 35 miles per hour (56 km/hr), heavy snow, and temperatures below −20°F (−29°C) all at the same time. In a "whiteout," a combination of snow and low cloud makes it impossible to see the horizon. Such conditions make you disoriented, and it's easy to get lost or injured. Cattle caught in a blizzard will shuffle backward until they reach the nearest solid structure—a fence or the wall of a barn—then wait it out.

HURRICANES

When tropical seas reach at least 80°F (27°C), a current of warm, moist air rushes up to heat the air above them, creating low pressure at the surface. If trade winds rush into this low-pressure area they can create a rising spiral of wind. The earth's rotation causes this spiral to twist, forming a storm system. This is known as a tropical storm until the wind speeds exceed 73 miles per hour (117 km/hr) when it officially becomes known as a hurricane in the Atlantic, a typhoon in the western Pacific, and a cyclone in the Indian Ocean. One of the most dangerous storm systems known to humans, a hurricane will set off on its course, continuing to build strength for as long as it is fueled by warm seas.

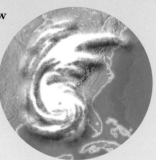

▷ **Hurricane Andrew**
This satellite map shows Hurricane Andrew striking Florida and the Gulf states in August 1992. It killed 23 people and the cleanup cost was $20.5 billion.

▽ **Speed of travel**
Hurricanes move at 20–30 miles per hour (32–48 km/hr) and can travel 300–400 miles (480–645 km) a day.

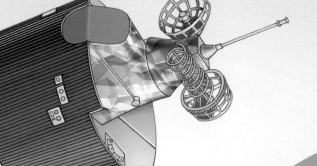

△ **Meanwhile, up in orbit**
Weather satellites look for clusters of thunderstorms over tropical oceans and monitor them for any signs of rotation.

Average air pressure at sea level is 1,013.25 millibars; in the eye of the storm, it can be less than 900.

WHERE DO THEY OCCUR?

Hurricanes, typhoons, and cyclones form between 5° and 23.5° north and south of the Equator and tend to move westward (because of the trade winds) and slightly toward the poles. Hurricane season is from June to November north of the Equator, while in the south it's from November to March.

HURRICANE ALERT!

The first sign that a hurricane is on the way might be a large sea swell while there is little wind. The wind and rain will get more intense as the storm gets closer. The area right in the center of a hurricane, where the air pressure is lowest, is known as the eye, and people on the ground will experience this as a calm stillness. However, the wall surrounding the eye brings the fiercest gusts and heaviest rain.

▽ Categories
There are five strengths of hurricane; category 5 winds are over 155 miles per hour (250 km/hr).

◁ ▽ Typhoons
Typhoons, which batter the coasts of Taiwan and Japan in season, are as destructive as hurricanes. During World War II, American sailors had to return to port in an aircraft carrier with a prow badly buckled by a typhoon.

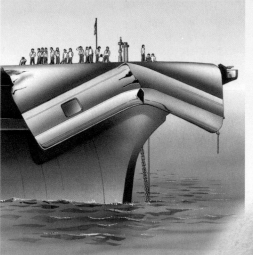

NAMES

Male or female?
• At first hurricanes were named after saints' days, then during World War II meteorologists named them after their girlfriends (Peaches and Hot Lips, for example). Now they give them alphabetical names starting with A each season and alternating between male and female ones. X, Y, and Z aren't used, so if they pass W in a season they switch to the Greek alphabet.

◁ Size-wise
Hurricanes can be 600 miles (965 km) across.

STORM SURGE
The storm surge connected with a hurricane is likely to cause more damage and loss of life than the winds and rain. A mound of water is sucked up into the eye of the hurricane and builds up as the ocean floor rises toward the land. The more gradual the slope, the greater the storm surge. With a category 5 hurricane, a mound of water as high as 18 feet (5.5 meters) can surge ashore. As the hurricane moves away from the sea, its source of energy lessens and it fades fast, but rain may continue for several days.

◁ In a spin
Around the eye, warm air rises to create fast rotating winds.

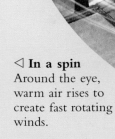
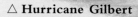

△ Hurricane Gilbert
In September 1988, Hurricane Gilbert made 750,000 people homeless along the Texan, Mexican, and Caribbean coasts. A Cuban fishing boat that had been anchored at sea smashed through a hotel in Cancun, Mexico.

TWISTERS

We've seen what happens when spiral storms form over tropical seas—but what happens when they occur over land? The result can be the world's deadliest storms, known as tornadoes or twisters, with wind speeds faster than 300 miles per hour (480 km/hr). Anything in their path can be sucked up and deposited miles away: cars, livestock, buildings, even people. When you read peculiar news stories about fish or frogs raining from the sky, you can be fairly sure a tornado was responsible. The U.S. is the world's most tornado-prone country, with storms tending to occur in the Great Plains in May or June. However, freak tornadoes can occur almost anywhere in the world when the atmospheric conditions are right.

△ **Funnel clouds**
Not all funnel clouds touch down on the ground. When they do, their movement is erratic, like a child's spinning top swerving here and there. In a row of three homes they can demolish the two on each side but leave the center home completely unharmed.

▷ **How they form**
Tornadoes form in areas where cool, dry air from the north meets warm, moist air from the south. Huge cumulonimbus clouds form, a funnel of cool air sinks down, and warm air spirals up inside it. Strong winds set up the horizontal rotation and force it into a violent spin.

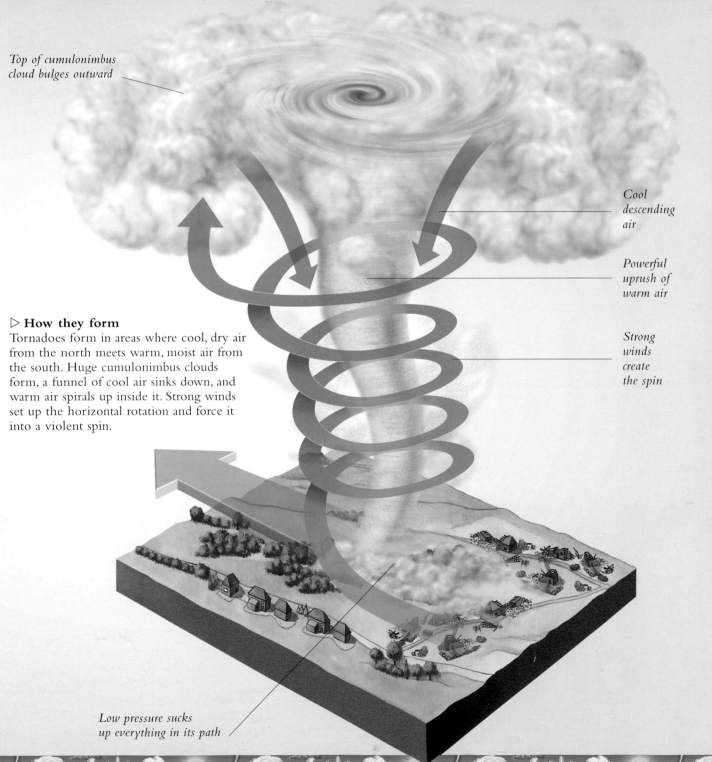

Top of cumulonimbus cloud bulges outward

Cool descending air

Powerful uprush of warm air

Strong winds create the spin

Low pressure sucks up everything in its path

◁ Exploding buildings
The difference between the extremely low air pressure in the center of a tornado and the higher pressure inside a building can cause the building to explode outward.

TORNADO ODDITIES

- Tornadoes can do some very strange things. In a storm in Oklahoma City in 1999, winds of 380 miles per hour (610 km/hr) ripped a baby from its mother's arms. She searched frantically until the baby was found unharmed in bushes 100 feet (30 meters) away.

- You never know what you'll find when you're clearing up—cars can be inside the house instead of the garage.

- For many years, observers were puzzled by the discovery that chickens caught up in tornadoes seemed to have all their feathers plucked. Was the powerful force of the low-pressure vortex pulling out their feathers? Animal experts had a different explanation—that chickens tend to molt when they are very stressed—and there can't be many more stressful moments in a chicken's life than being swept up by a tornado!

△ Sandstorms
Grains of sand are heavy and cause a lot of damage when they are lifted into the air by a storm. They knock down telegraph poles, strip the paint from vehicles, and they are responsible for eroding the features of Egypt's Great Sphinx of Giza.

◁ Waterspouts
When tornadoes form over the ocean, they create waterspouts, which move along slowly in a curved path, causing a dangerous hazard to ships and small boats. The water in a tornado is not sucked up from the surface, though—it is mostly the result of condensation caused by the very low pressure inside the spiral. In 1956 in Chilatchee, Alabama, a woman and her husband witnessed a very strange event. As they watched from their backyard, a small dark cloud in the otherwise clear blue sky above them suddenly released hundreds of fish—catfish, bass, and bream— all of them still alive. The only explanation for such a unusual downpour can be that the fish had been sucked up by a whirlwind of some sort as it traveled across the creeks and rivers in the area.

OCEAN CURRENTS

Water continually flows around the world's oceans, from the Atlantic to the Indian to the Pacific, and back to the Atlantic. The entire circuit takes a single drop of water 500 to 2,000 years! Scientists believe that sea temperatures and the extent of the polar ice caps are the best clues for predicting long-range weather patterns. In particular, the water temperature in the South Pacific controls many aspects of global weather and it can cause severe droughts, flooding, hurricanes and volcanoes, when the waters warm or cool by just a few degrees from the normal range.

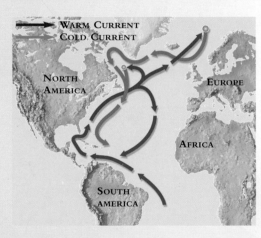

WARM CURRENT
COLD CURRENT

NORTH AMERICA

EUROPE

AFRICA

SOUTH AMERICA

◁ **What if... ?**
Some scientists think the effects of global warming could stop the Greenland Pump working during the 21st century. If it does, there might be ice skating around the Statue of Liberty one day.

◁ **Vacation surprise**
El Niños affect the trade winds, producing extreme weather in the tropics and more typhoons and hurricanes.

An El Niño event brings heavy rainfall and storms as cumulonimbus clouds form over the ocean

WESTERN PACIFIC
The easterly trade winds lessen or even stop completely

AUSTRALIA

Temperatures in the western Pacific are normally 14°F (8°C) hotter than in the east, but during an El Niño the water gets warmer off South America

N

△ Gulf Stream
The Gulf Stream takes a warm surface current from the Caribbean up the east coast of the U.S. and on to the North Atlantic, where it mingles with colder, saltier water, cools itself, and sinks down in a system known as the Greenland Pump, to be recycled back down south. Without it, the climates of New York and London would be more like that of Newfoundland.

EL NIÑO
El Niño is a warm ocean current that appears off the northwest coast of Peru around Christmas. However, roughly every two to seven years it appears much further south than usual, causing what is known as an El Niño event. The trade winds weaken and sea temperatures rise, resulting in severe ripple effects on weather around the world, from Australia to western Europe and North America.

▷ The 1997-98 El Niño

This powerful El Niño event caused one of the warmest and wettest winters and springs on record in the U.S. and Canada, as well as a particularly deadly tornado season during April 1998.

▽ Fishing

The ocean food chain works when fish can feed in cold, salty, nutrient-rich waters. An increase of just 1°F (0.6°C) for three months kills fish and plankton, which in turn kills fish-eating seabirds. South American fishermen are among the first to know of an El Niño event.

△ Drought

During the dramatic 1982–83 El Niño event there was a record-breaking drought that killed 340 people in Indonesia, cut Australia's grain production in half, and led to hundreds of livestock perishing, at a cost of $2.5 billion.

It tends to be dry in the Americas during a La Niña, with excessive rainfall in Asia and Australia

The trade winds strengthen during a La Niña

EASTERN PACIFIC

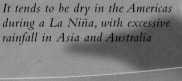

SOUTH AMERICA

Sea surface temperatures off South America become much colder than usual while the western Pacific gets warmer

LA NIÑA

Major El Niño events can last three to four years and are followed by La Niña, when ocean temperatures are colder than normal. The impact of La Niña on global weather is the opposite of El Niño. Both events cause extremes of weather—more torrential rain and flooding creating mud slides, more hurricanes and tornadoes, more severe heat leading to wildfires, and more unsettled winters.

◁ Two extremes

The wind, rain, and sea temperature patterns for a La Niña event are shown here; a typical El Niño event is shown on page 24.

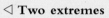

△ Heavy rains in the U.S.

A very stormy period in California in the winter of 2004–05 was due to a weak El Niño event, as well as a blocking pattern along the West Coast that trapped the weather. Heavy rain and hail combined with high snowfall in central California. Too many events like this could cause mud slides and put certain major landmarks at risk!

EXTREME WEATHER

There may be a severe storm somewhere in the world at any given moment, but when it coincides with another weather system or local geographical weakness, the results can be catastrophic. What causes such extreme disasters? One theory is that the atmosphere is so sensitive that something as simple as a butterfly flapping its wings in Tokyo, producing a tiny movement of air, could have ripple effects that culminate in ice storms over New York, tornadoes over London, and cyclones in the Bay of Bengal. We've only been keeping systematic weather records since the 19th century; imagine what might have been going on before then.

KRAKATOA, 1883

When Krakatoa erupted in 1883, the explosion from the volcano was so loud that it was heard over one-twelfth of the planet. It created a 130-foot (40-meter) tidal wave, and so much rock was blasted into the atmosphere and circulated in the jet streams that the earth cooled by almost 1°F (0.6°C). Evening skies were colored blood-red for the next five years.

◁ **New Orleans, 2005**
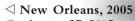
On August 27, 2005, Hurricane Katrina didn't hit New Orleans directly, but the effects of its 200-mile-an-hour (320-km/hr) winds on Lake Pontchartrain were like someone tipping it on its end. Water pounded along the levees, breaching them in several places and leaving 80 percent of the city under water.

△ **Volcanic eruptions**
The clouds of ash and dust can lower global temperatures, because they reflect solar radiation back into space. They can also produce "acid rain," which damages trees and vegetation.

◁ **Bangladesh, 1970**
Bangladesh is a low-lying country fed by three major rivers, so it's always at risk of flooding during the monsoon season. In 1970, this combined with the worst cyclone in recorded history to form 50-foot (15-meter) waves and 150-mile-an-hour (240-km/hr) winds that overwhelmed the region and killed up to 500,000 people.

◁ The perfect storm, 1991
On October 28, 1991, a cold front moving down from Canada developed a low-pressure system over the northeastern U.S. Hurricane Grace, traveling up from the Caribbean, made a hairpin turn to combine forces with this low. Extremely high tides were the third factor in the "perfect storm" that developed, with hurricane-force winds and waves of 30 feet (9 meters) or more. The fishing boat *Andrea Gail* disappeared off Newfoundland, and there was damage costing hundreds of millions of dollars to buildings along the northeast coastline.

△ Tristate tornado, 1925
The most devastating tornado in recorded history destroyed the towns of Annapolis (Missouri), Gorham (Illinois), and Griffin, and a quarter of Princeton (Indiana). The death toll was 695, and 15,000 homes were destroyed in the storm's 219-mile (350-km), 3½-hour rampage.

▷ Tsunamis
These powerful waves travel great distances at high speed. They can be caused by earthquakes, volcanic eruptions, landslides, and even by asteroids landing in the ocean.

ASIAN TSUNAMI, 2004
On December 26, 2004, a tsunami devastated areas bordering the Indian Ocean. It had been triggered by an underwater earthquake measuring a massive 9 on the Richter scale. The energy released was equivalent to 14 Hiroshima bombs, and so powerful that it caused the earth to wobble on its axis by about 1 inch (2.5 cm), shortening our average daylight hours by three-millionths of a second. This may not sound like much, but it could have a significant effect on world agriculture and weather patterns.

WEATHER STATS

Record-breakers
- Hottest: 136°F (58°C), Libya, September 13, 1922.
- Coldest: −126.8°F (−88°C), Antarctica, July 21, 1983.
- Driest: Atacama Desert, Chile, with an average annual rainfall of 0.003 inches (0.007 cm).
- Wettest: 73½ inches (187 cm), Réunion, Indian Ocean, March 15, 1952.
- Fastest recorded wind speed: 231 mph (370 km/hr), Mount Washington, New Hampshire, April 12, 1934.
- Deepest snowfall: 37 feet 7 inches (11.5 meters), Tamarack, California, March 1911.

FUTURE WEATHER

The earth's climate has gotten warmer by 1°F (0.6°C) over the past 100 years, and it seems to be because we have more carbon dioxide (CO_2) in our atmosphere, trapping the sun's heat. Unfortunately, global warming doesn't mean we will have sunnier weather; many experts believe that we're entering a period when we will have more extreme weather. That's right: more heavy rain, thunderstorms, hurricanes, and tornadoes. Weather may be getting harder to predict, and meteorologists often seem to get it wrong, so don't ignore the old-fashioned methods described on the opposite page, particularly when it comes to forecasting storms.

Areas of Europe threatened by flooding if the ice caps continue to melt at the current rate

△ **Rising sea levels**
If we do nothing to cut back on CO_2 production, scientists think the earth could be up to 8°F (4.5°C) warmer by 2060, which would mean larger areas of the polar ice caps melting and the world's sea levels rising by more than 3 feet (1 meter). This would put New York and London under water.

△ **Melting ice caps**
Temperatures at the poles are rising faster than in the rest of the world, causing the ice caps to melt. In 2002 in the Antarctic, the Larsen B ice shelf—1,200 square miles (3,100 sq km)—fell into the sea, making it difficult for penguins to reach their feeding grounds. In the north, Baffin Bay is thawing earlier each year, forcing polar bears to change their migration routes.

THE GREENHOUSE EFFECT
When heat from the sun enters the earth's atmosphere, some is reflected by clouds, while the rest warms the earth's surface before going back into space. However, greenhouse gases (a mixture of CO_2, methane, and CFCs or chlorofluorocarbons) absorb and give out this heat. We are creating too many greenhouse gases by burning fossil fuels for electricity and using it to power vehicles and airplanes. These gases trap more of the sun's heat in the earth's atmosphere, so global temperatures are gradually rising.

◁ **Ozone layer**
The ozone layer protects us from harmful ultraviolet rays. In the 1980s, a hole was found in the ozone above the Antarctic; it is thought this was caused by aircraft fuel and chloroflurocarbons (CFCs) in foam plastic packaging, aerosols, and refrigerators. The most harmful CFCs are now banned, but there is evidence of a smaller ozone hole over the Arctic and another over Australia and New Zealand.

DEFORESTATION

The earth's forests absorb CO_2 and release oxygen into the atmosphere. Cutting down too many trees could ultimately make the earth uninhabitable. Destroying the rain forests causes higher daytime temperatures and lower nighttime ones, while cutting down trees in snowy climates makes them much cooler.

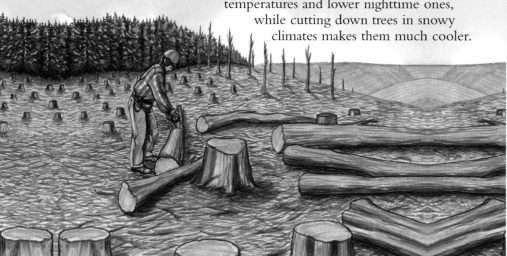

△ Folk wisdom #1
Since 1886, a groundhog has been brought out of hibernation every February 2 in Punxsutawney, Pennsylvania. According to tradition, if it sees its shadow, there are another 40 days of winter to come. If it doesn't, there will be an early spring.

△ Folk wisdom #2
"Goose honks high, weather fair; Goose honks low, weather foul."

▽ Folk wisdom #3
Some say you can estimate the air temperature by counting how many times crickets chirp in a minute. Researchers have come up with a formula you can try. Count the number of chirps made in 15 seconds, then add 37. This figure is an indication of the outside temperature in degrees Fahrenheit.

Dolphins playing on the surface of the water

STORM WARNING

Watch out for any of these signs, which could mean that a storm is on the way.

Birds going to roost

Ducks quacking more than usual

Horses shying

Bees staying close to the hive

Frogs croaking more than usual

Ants marching in a straight line

GLOSSARY AND INDEX

air pressure The weight of the atmosphere over a particular part of the earth.

barometer An instrument for measuring air pressure.

Beaufort scale A scale that categorizes winds according to their strength.

butterfly effect The idea that an event as small as a butterfly flapping its wings can affect global weather.

CFCs (chlorofluorocarbons) Gases given off by certain industrial processes that interfere with the ozone layer in the upper levels of the atmosphere.

cold front The front edge of a mass of cold air.

convectional rain Rain caused by warm air masses rising into the atmosphere.

Coriolis force The effect of the planet's rotation on wind direction.

cumulonimbus clouds Large rain-bearing clouds that stretch from low to high levels of the atmosphere and often bring thunderstorms.

cyclone (1) The name for a hurricane in the Indian Ocean; (2) a moving low-pressure mass of air; also known as a depression.

depression A moving low-pressure mass of air that often brings rain; also known as a cyclone.

doldrums A belt of calm around the Equator where sailing ships can become stuck through lack of wind.

downdraft A downward movement of cool air.

drought Lower-than-average rainfall in an area for a prolonged period.

El Niño A warm ocean current flowing down the west coast of South America; fluctuations in this current can cause extreme global weather changes.

flash floods Floods caused by intense rainfall in a local area, which the soil is unable to absorb; they are most common in valleys and gorges.

funnel cloud A whirling column of cloud reaching down from a cumulonimbus cloud.

global warming The rise in the temperature of the earth's atmosphere.

greenhouse effect The way certain gases trap heat in the earth's atmosphere.

Gulf Stream A circulating ocean current that takes warm water from the Gulf of Mexico to the North Atlantic and returns colder, saltier water south.

horse latitudes High-pressure areas found around 30°N and 30°S.

humidity The amount of water vapor in the air.

isobars Lines on a weather map connecting points with the same air pressure at a particular time.

jet stream Fast-moving winds high in the atmosphere.

La Niña A cooling of the El Niño ocean current, which causes global weather changes.

leeward Direction toward which the wind blows.

megalightning Powerful bursts of above-cloud lightning.

monsoon The rainy season in Southeast Asia, from about April to October.

occluded front A weather front created when a warm front is forced upward by a cold front.

ozone A layer of gas in the upper atmosphere that absorbs harmful ultraviolet rays from the sun.

Richter scale A scale describing the size of earthquakes based on how much energy they release.

storm surge A body of water driven onshore during a hurricane.

supercooled water Water droplets with a temperature below freezing, which are still in liquid form.

temperate zones The parts of the world between the Arctic Circle and the Tropic of Cancer, and between the Antarctic Circle and the Tropic of Capricorn.

trade winds The prevailing winds in the tropics.

transpiration The process in which plants give off water vapor into the atmosphere.

tropics The area between the Tropic of Cancer (23.5°N) and the Tropic of Capricorn (23.5°S).

tsunami A huge wave caused by earthquakes, volcanic eruptions, or other geographical phenomena; not a tidal wave, which is caused by high winds and spring tides.

typhoon The name given to a hurricane in the western Pacific or the China Sea.

updraft A strong movement of air up from the ground.

warm front The front edge of a mass of warm air.

weather blocker A geographical feature (usually mountains) that stops the movement of weather systems.

weather satellite An instrument in orbit around the planet that detects meteorological phenomena.